Your Free Gift

I wanted to show my appreciation that you support my work so I've put together a free gift for you.

Business Startup Resource Toolkit

Just visit the link below to download it now.

http://zenmagicpublishing.com/hbb

Thanks!

Zachary Grayson

Introduction

In a generation where getting a job is a daunting task, people are constantly trying to find a way to get by on their own. Plus, a stereotypical 9 to 5 job is just not that appealing anymore and people are beginning to realize that there are other options for supporting oneself.

The truth is, there are plenty of ways to make a living without having to work for someone else eight hours a day. It is possible to live a quality life managing your own business, no matter the experience or skills you have. Anything can be learned, everything is taught and with the right amount of passion, hard work and ambition, your biggest goals and dreams can be reached.

This book is aimed at people like you who are ready to start a new chapter in your life, who are tired of doing the same thing every day and who simply want to change their ways for a better future. The reality is that, especially in this day and age, there are plenty of occupations that don't require you to be confined within your boss' limitations. Anyone can step away from the pack and quite honestly; it's not that difficult, although, it will take a substantial amount of work and dedication on your part.

In this book, I will introduce to you a number of opportunities you can grab hold of that don't require working 9 to 5. I will explain what each opportunity will bring to you, how you can get started, what skills you will need to excel, things to expect when you begin and how to maintain it, some ideas on how to expand your business and lastly some tips on how to make the most of your business.

My personal goal for this book is to help people just like you realize that you don't need to live a life full of taking orders from someone else. I want people to know that there are other ways to live and not only succeed in their business, but have fun doing it. Life doesn't have to be boring. We are capable of paving our own roads to success and it's getting more popular and more common each and every day.

As you read on and take in the many tips and information I am going to share with you, remember that these are all opportunities in which anyone can excel. Any skills or experience needed can be learned.

I hope you enjoy the insight I am about to share with you and use this information to your advantage. I wish you the best of luck in your journey and hope you exceed your own expectations. Remember: Nothing is guaranteed to be easy, but anything is possible with determination.

I. Internet Retail

Home-based internet businesses are becoming more and more popular. The truth is, anyone can start a business based solely on the internet. The problem is, not everyone is going to make money with a home-based internet business. The main reason for this is because starting, maintaining and becoming successful with an internet business takes a lot of learning and hard work. People aren't prepared to face that and end up getting frustrated and give up too early.

Before you create an internet business, be prepared to work hard and open to learning new skills. All the ways to succeed may appear simple, but that is no guarantee that they will be easy.

Introduction

eBay is a great way to grow a business in the comfort of your own home. If you are capable of selling items online, then this would be a great place to start and make a name for yourself. It's a very simple and easy way to sell items to customers around the world.

One of the biggest tips one can learn when beginning an online business, especially if you want to be a successful, is to remember that going where the customers are is your most valuable weapon. If you are looking to sell items, then eBay is the place to go. It is one of the leading websites in the online auction market. It's where the customers are, which means it's where your online business needs to be.

What Can You Do?

eBay brings a lot of tools to your fingertips, making it easier for you to sell products/items at a fast rate. The existing web presence and storefront makes it easy for owners without a lot of experience in web design or who lack the capital needed to start an online retail business. Instead you can use that money to purchase inventory or shipping supplies.

What eBay does is bring you everything needed to run an online retail business in one place. What things? With eBay, you can easily list items to be sold in an auction format or a "Buy It Now" format. This helps you manage your inventory in an organized way and also helps you keep track of sales made. It allows you to open an online store right on their site, making it easy for you to manage an online retailing business.

Making it easier for business owners to sell, ship and manage posted inventory is what eBay thrives upon. If you're looking for an easy way to open, manage and maintain an online store, eBay will give you all the necessary tools to do so.

How To Get Started

When opening an online store with eBay, there are a lot of things for which to prepare. These are the things you should do before you begin to sell on the site.

First, you should start by thinking of what kind of products you would like to sell. Ultimately, you can sell anything and everything. Whether you want to stick to a certain type of product or hold yourself to no limitations is up to you. However, it is very important to figure out what you want to sell before you dig into your business. Once you figure out the kind of products you'll be selling, then you should think of a name for your business that corresponds with what you sell.

Next, you should gather inventory to sell. You can start small with some things around the house or you can search for deals on your product that you can buy in bulk. When you get enough inventory, make sure to store it in one place, wherever that may be. After you get product, make sure you gather shipping material as well. You will need envelopes of all sizes, boxes, tape, etc. all depending on product size and fragility.

Once you have your shipping materials, work on getting quality photographs of your products. These will be used later when you post your product to the eBay site. Make sure they are of good quality and show the item from all angles so the customers know exactly what they will be receiving. Save the pictures in a folder where you can easily access them.

Next on the list, you will need to open up an eBay seller account. This can be done by first signing up on the eBay home page (www.eBay.com). Once you open up an account, access the "Start Selling" page to post items immediately. If you have a larger inventory and plan on doing this long-term, then you should open an eBay storefront. This will help you post more products at a faster rate. There are different types of storefronts, depending on how much you plan on selling. Choose the option most relevant to your business.

Now, you are ready to start selling on eBay. Post a product on the eBay website and wait for someone to buy your item. You can increase your chances of being seen by promoting and marketing your products or storefront. You can do this through social media, e-mail or just simply word of mouth. After that, all you have to do is maintain inventory and make sure you have constant inventory to sell.

What To Expect
First off, here are some startup costs and expenses you should look out for. Obviously, you need to buy inventory. You don't have to start off large. Begin with a few products and aim to make a profit off those. More profit means more freedom to buy additional inventory. More products means more profit. In addition to that, if you open up an eBay storefront, you will need to pay for that as well. The cost of a storefront depends on the size of the store you open. A Basic Store costs $20 per month, a Premium Store costs $60 per month and an Anchor Store costs $200 per month.

Next, let's talk income. As you would expect, income is based on how much you sell. If you only sell a small list of products, then you probably won't be making much profit. That's usually the case at startup. You need to realize that it won't be an instant moneymaker. Like I said above, larger inventory means larger profit. However, after you make a name for yourself on eBay, sellers can easily make a living off of this method. This isn't something that you can work on a couple times a week. It's something that should be maintained daily. Be prepared to work very hard, especially at the start. Be patient.

Additional Tips

Once you start selling, you will realize that customers will leave feedback for you. They will rate their experience with you and it will be available for future customers to view. This is very important. If you maintain a high rating, then customers will trust you and be more inclined to buy from you. However, if your rating steeps too low, you will find yourself struggling to find customers. You will be rated on how accurately you advertise your product and how quickly and safely you pack it for mailing. It's very easy to maintain a high rating by being honest and truthful in all your dealings.

One last tip: Think carefully about how you list your item. This includes everything from the category you place your product under, to the description, title and photographs you use when listing your product. Make sure everything is appealing to the customer. Explain to them why they should buy from you and not someone else. Simply put, sell your product as if you're the one buying it. Place yourself in the buyers' shoes.

Amazon Marketplace

Introduction

Another way to sell product online is through Amazon. Similar to eBay, Amazon allows you to manage an online store conveniently in one place. They have a vast array of tools that make selling on the internet very simple.

Amazon and eBay can go hand in hand when opening an internet retail business. Essentially, you can use one or both to your advantage. Amazon uses the same concepts as eBay just a different website. One tool that can be used on Amazon is called Fulfillment. This allows you to eliminate the shipping process to individual buyers, which, in return, saves you valuable time. With Fulfillment, all you have to do is send your inventory in bulk directly to Amazon. From that point, Amazon handles the picking, packing and shipping to the customer so you don't have to deal with it. Pretty cool, right?

How To Get Started

Getting started on Amazon is similar to getting started on eBay. Before anything, you need to prepare yourself with inventory, shipping materials and the storage space to hold inventory.

Next, you're going to need to set up an account with Amazon. If you are looking to build a business out of it, which you probably are, then it is recommended you open an Amazon Webstore. This is similar to eBay's Storefront. It allows you to manage inventory and keep track of sales.

Once you open up your Webstore, it is time to start selling. This is simply done by listing your products in the database. Remember to make your listings appealing to the customer. Take high-resolution photos that show the item clearly. Be truthful in your description. The time you take to present your product well will be a benefit in the long run. It will pave the way for positive feedback that ultimately builds your credibility in the Amazon Marketplace.

After you list your inventory, you need to maintain your business by constantly buying new inventory based on what's selling. If something isn't selling, decrease the price. If something is selling well, try increasing the price a little and make sure to keep that product in stock. If the market demands a higher quality product, one that is brighter, shinier or bigger, keep that in mind when you restock your inventory.

What To Expect

Expenses are going to be similar to those for eBay. First, you're going to need inventory. Depending on what you're selling, this expense can be high or low. Your main goal when buying product is to make sure you can make a profit on it. Buying in bulk usually helps you save money, in return, making you bigger profit (Win-Win).

Unlike eBay's Storefronts, Amazon's Webstore cost is one flat rate every month. It does not offer the flexibility found on eBay where you can choose the size of your Storefront. It's simply $79 per month. An additional feature of Amazon is the ability to promote your products with ads throughout the site. The cost of ads is in addition to the monthly fee.

For a reminder, starting and maintaining an online retail store will take a lot of time and work. Be prepared for a lot of long nights that will require a lot of patience. Profit may not come in abundance at first, but always keep a goal in mind that will help you to strive to do better. There's no such thing as having too large of a goal, it only pushes you to reach higher heights.

Additional Tips

This tip bears repeating: If you want to save time, take part in Fulfillment by Amazon. As I said before, enlisting in this tool will save you lot of time. Amazon will personally pick, pack and ship your products once sold. This allows you to spend more time listing items and buying inventory.

Another helpful tip, which is also found in eBay, is to conduct your business in such a way that will keep buyers leaving you positive feedback. Give your customers what you advertise and don't promise them things you can't deliver. If you are going to handle shipping yourself, try to ship your products as fast as you can. Remember: Positive feedback means more customers will be inclined to buy from you. Be responsive and available to your customers. Some people may have questions for you. Prompt responses breed positive results. Pay attention to feedback you receive and respond as appropriate.

II. Freelance

Freelance is defined as a self-employed person working or available to work, for a number of employers, who are usually hired for a limited period of time. There are plenty of jobs you can get on the internet that are considered freelance. For the most part, the sky is the limit if you are a freelancer. I will share with you a couple of opportunities in the freelance area that can easily be turned into a career.

One of the best things about freelancing is that you can pretty much pick up any skill needed to complete the job. That's what I meant by the sky is the limit. You can be working for ten different employers doing ten different things. If its variety you crave, then this may be the genre for you.

Blogging

Introduction

The best way to describe blogging is that it's a diary on the internet that is frequently updated, sometimes daily. Blog content can be about anything; from car maintenance, fitness goals, travel notes or household tips. The newer aspect of blogging is that it can be used to generate income. Blogging requires commitment, attention and topics that attract crowds of people. It also has the potential to turn into a career, to the point where you can quit your day job and support yourself doing something you love. In addition, it is a great way to express your feelings over the internet, keeping in mind that it will be available for the whole world to see.

How To Start

I think the first thing to do when you want to start blogging is to figure out what you'll be blogging about. You can pick anything, whatever makes you feel inspired. Basically, pick a topic that you'll never get tired of writing about because believe me, you'll be writing about this genre A LOT.

After you get all of that planned, you should start getting a site together. There are plenty of options to choose from. If you want a simple blog without a lot of plugins, you can use Wix, Blogger, Wordpress or Weebly to create a quick, free website. If you want something more complex, you can use Wordpress and Blogger to purchase exclusive plugins to make your site more appealing.

Once your site is live, just start writing about your genre. If you chose to write about sports, then write about your opinions on current events happening in the sports world. Do this for about six months. Rule of thumb is to post about 3 new entries per week.

After you get your site filled with content and start to get a following, place ads on your site to help bring in some income. You can use Google ads and sign up for AdSense, or use BlogAds or CrispAds. The way these work is that you, the site owner, signs up with an ad placement service of your choice, create a blank space or bucket on your site. When a visitor is viewing your site an ad will show up in that bucket based on what subject(s) the viewer has searched on the internet.

Once you have ads on the site, apply to a blog network. Some companies include: b5Media, 451 press and Wise Bread. When they ask you if you would like to create a new topic, check and make sure they don't already have a topic that you picked. If not, suggest the topic and wait for approval.

After that, it's time to start searching for other blogging jobs. Now that you have some experience to display to employers, you can start competing for jobs to increase your income. There are several places you can go to for blogging jobs. A main source is the *Pro Blogger Job Board* where you can apply for certain positions posted there. Be aware, though, only take on as much work as you think you can handle.

After you have a couple blogging jobs, you will begin to build a portfolio. The larger and more varied your portfolio, the more chance you have of landing bigger jobs. Soon enough, you could see yourself making a lot of money.

What To Expect

First, let's talk about what kind of skills you'll need. Computer skills are a must as well as knowing how to use programs like, Microsoft Word and Microsoft Excel. In addition, most websites use Wordpress to post blogs, so if you're going to be working for other people, a brief understanding of how to post using Wordpress would be recommended. Other than that, it's just you typing out your personal thoughts.

As far as startup costs and expenses go, there isn't really much. You will need a computer, so if you don't already own one, that could be one expense. If you're someone who likes to brainstorm on paper, then paper and a pen will be needed. Other than that, you won't really need much.

Lastly, let's talk about the time commitment involved. To be completely honest, you're going to need to dedicate a lot of time to become a full time blogger. I would recommend spending at least 2 hours per day, Monday through Friday just on writing. Research time would be additional. If you have multiple blogging jobs that time would increase. Consider the time you devote to blogging as an investment in your future.

Additional Notes
My first tip is to suggest making money through affiliate marketing. Essentially, it means that you promote someone else's product and earn a commission if they purchase said product. Companies like Amazon, ClickBank and Commission Junction all offer easy affiliate marketing platforms. Sign up with any of these companies and watch your blog make more income than before.

Another tip is going to be repeated due to its importance. Be prepared to dedicate a lot of time to the upkeep of your blog. At first, I would attempt to secure as many jobs as you can. Do your best to impress these employers. They can be used as references in the future and the experience will help you climb the blogging ladder a lot faster. Trust me, the extra time put in will go a long way in the end.

Virtual Assistant

Introduction
If you are someone that is very good at customer service or someone that's on the phone a lot, then this might spark your interest. This job requires you to basically be someone's assistant without actually physically being near them. All of your assistant duties will be handled either on the computer or by phone.

This is a good job for someone who loves working from home, has excellent communication skills and a knack for computer work. Plus, if you prove to be very good as a virtual assistant, then you could find yourself working for some big name businesses and getting paid nicely in return.

How To Get Started
First of all, you will need to decide what services you would like to offer to your employers. For the most part, this will be a variety of secretarial skills. However, the market for virtual assistants is growing and they are now being asked to do other things like web design, ghost writing or translation services.

After you choose what you are offering, give yourself a quick evaluation. If you need any practice or need to acquire any skills to make sure you perform to the best of your abilities, then find online classes for help. It is important to know how to perform the skills you advertise. This will make things go smoothly and will increase your confidence.

Once you feel confident in yourself, it is recommended, but not mandatory, that you take a virtual assistant certification program. Assistu and Virtual Assistant Worldwide Certification are companies that offer certification programs. They also offer training to prepare you to take their test.

After you have all of that, it's time to start finding work. You can find these kinds of jobs on websites like oDesk, Guru and Freelancer. You'll need to create a profile, stating your experience, education and skill sets. Having sample work to put in your portfolio is essential. Prospective employers want to see samples of previous work before they decide to hire someone. Start searching for job postings in the virtual assistant (VA) category. If you don't have work samples to post, consider doing work at a low rate in order to build your portfolio. Specific, positive feedback from employers is another way to demonstrate your abilities and will aid in getting hired for new jobs.

What To Expect

Much like blogging, becoming a virtual assistant won't require a lot of expenses or startup costs. You will need a phone, computer and most likely some kind of scanner. Once you have those things, you are ready to become a virtual assistant. Also, if you aren't familiar with programs like Microsoft Word, Microsoft PowerPoint and Microsoft Excel, then it is recommended to take classes to learn them.

As far as income goes, it's similar to blogging. You might start out slow, but that's normal. You will need to dedicate a lot of time to this business and won't see results right away. However, all of the hard work will pay off and you could see yourself with a business generating quite a bit of income.

Additional Notes

The first tip I'll give you on becoming a virtual assistant is to make sure you know how to use the programs that they will require you to use. Don't promote your skills for software you don't know. Nothing is worse than being given a project using a program you've never used before. If you feel your skill set is lacking it's very easy to take an online course to learn new software applications. Remain open to learn new things and your repertoire will continually expand.

My last tip is to always be nice. Speak in a professional manner, make all your work neat and organized and never make yourself seem unprepared. When you're working as an assistant to someone, you are there to make his or her life easier. If you end up making their life more stressful and difficult, then you won't get hired.

Introduction

Social media has infiltrated our daily lives. Even if you did not grow up with access to Facebook, Twitter, Pintrest, Tumblr, email and the like, chances are you connect with at least one of these social media sites every day. You're probably aware that keeping up with social media on a personal level takes time. Imagine trying to keep up with social media as a business. All of these channels of communication require attention. Businesses benefit from having a presence on social media. It provides multiple, critical marketing opportunities. This has created the need for people who can manage those streams of communication and they are aptly titled a social media manager.

As social media changes the world, it's also making some people quite a bit of money. Why not make money doing something you do every day? Sounds too good to be true, right? Well, it's real and it's pretty much available to anyone willing to step up to the plate. It's a very simple job that will require a lot of organizational skills.

The best part about this job is that it is pretty much recession-proof. New businesses are created every day. These businesses need to market themselves. Social media helps with that, so every business is in need of a person to control that.

How To Get Started

Whether you have been active with social media your whole life or are new to the world of social media, I would recommend taking a social media course before beginning. These courses teach everything from using sites like Facebook, blogging, email marketing and other aspects connected to this job. You can find these courses online at some colleges and universities, as well as other websites you can find with a Google search.

This next step is for people who haven't yet been too active with social media. I recommend getting familiar with sites by setting up personal accounts for yourself. Maintain these profiles for a while so you get used to the various platforms. Become familiar with the specific nuances and limitations of the various media. This is your training so you're better prepared when you get a job as a social media manager.

After that, I would recommend creating a blog or write for someone else's blog. Create posts and use these to demonstrate your writing skills. Most employers looking for a social media manager will require writing samples from all applicants. In addition, they often have you write a blog post or articles for their site.

Next, it is also recommended to take online courses on marketing. Being informed and educated on marketing is a huge plus for a social media manager. Knowing how social media will affect the company's marketing campaign would be a huge advantage over most other people. Most of the time, employers will hire someone who knows marketing over someone who doesn't.

Once you've finished all of your research, training and testing on becoming a social media manager, it's time for you to find work. These jobs can be found on sites like oDesk, Fiverr, Guru and Elance. Search the category Social Media Management (SMM) and find a job that will compliment your skills positively. After you've made a name for yourself and built a good portfolio, jobs could come easily and income could become quite steady.

What To Expect

Like most freelance jobs and opportunities, you're not going to see a lot of expenses. When first starting, you'll need to make sure you have all the necessary technology. A desktop computer or laptop is required. A smartphone would also be useful, allowing you to do your work when you're on the run. In addition to that, any classes and training you take could cost you money, depending on where you go. Other than that, expenses will seem rare for this type of job.

As far as income goes, this could be a very steady income. Social media is becoming more and more popular, especially among businesses. These businesses are constantly looking for experts to manage their social media and raise their presence online. You have the opportunity to become one of these experts needed by almost every business.

Lastly, let's discuss the time required for this type of job. I believe at first, you will need to spend a lot of time building your name. However, you can save a lot of time when you're on the go. If you have a smartphone, you can always work while you're waiting for a bus or at the doctor's office. This can help you get work done a lot more quickly.

Additional Notes

When first starting out, I would highly suggest building profiles for yourself on all the major social media platforms. Make sure to post often on these platforms and build a nice following. This comes as an advantage when applying for jobs because you can show them your personal profiles as proof of what you are capable of doing. If you can show the employer that you get a lot of feedback on your profiles or have a nice following of people that read your stuff, you will be considered savvier than other applicants.

Another quick tip is to train yourself to be comfortable with any topic or niche. If you can handle a business' social media no matter the topic or kind of business it is, then you can find yourself highly sought after for work. Businesses like when someone is versatile, so do your best to show the employers everything you are capable of doing.

Website Design/Development

Introduction
There are thousands upon thousands of websites in existence today. Some are good, some are clunky and some are fantastic. What really goes into creating one of those fantastic sites? Is the desire to be cool and hip all you need to develop amazing websites that will wow your clients? Think again.

It's true there is work available for website designers and developers, but it's a buyer's market. If you are just starting out, know that this career path will require dedication, knowledge of many software applications, the ability to differentiate yourself from the competition and a keen business sense. I say this not to discourage you, but to be truthful.

How To Get Started
Okay, so I'm going to assume that anyone aspiring to become a website designer or developer already has a working knowledge of XHTML, CSS, web design standards, adobe creative suite, JavaScript and PHP. If you don't, however, then I would recommend you take the time to figure out what you need to learn and the cost involved in order to make an informed decision to move forward in this path.

Software knowledge is very important, but there are other skills you'll need that are just as important. For example, being able to effectively communicate with your customer, the ability to sell yourself, be open to feedback, stay up-to-date with the newest technology, and stay organized.

Once you decide this is the path for you, it's time to open up a web hosting account. It is very important that you make sure you choose an account that is capable of hosting several sites on that one account. This is the account you'll be using to host all of the websites you create.

Next, buy a web domain name for the website your business is going to have. Make sure the name is professional, yet engaging to the public. Also, make sure you make it clear that you are a web designer in the title. For example, something like "johndoewebdesign.com" would be perfect. Make it easy and simple so people can find you easily.

Once that is done, it's time to create your own website. I would suggest that your first step be to make a plan. Be thoughtful about your design and development.. Make sure it is the best work you've ever created because this is the most important work in your portfolio. Once businesses see not only how great the site looks but, more importantly, how easily your site can be navigated, they will want to consider you as a possible candidate to work on their website.

Once you have a website displaying your skills, it's time to start looking for work. Once again, you can use websites like oDesk, Guru, Elance and Fiverr to find jobs in this field. You can also make a name for yourself by contacting local businesses that currently don't have a website. This is where you need to be able to sell yourself confidently and show the prospective client why you are different from every other web designer. Obviously, you need to send them to your website to show off your talents.

Starting will be slow. You'll need to expand your portfolio. Experience is a great teacher. Consider doing some pro bono work in order to practice designing, learn about working with a client and finally, being able to add to your portfolio. There is work available, but you need to be able differentiate yourself from the crowd. Give prospective employers a reason to choose you over someone else. Exceed customers' expectations with every job you do. And, once you begin, never give up.

What To Expect

There are going to be some startup costs associated with this career path. When setting up your hosting account, you're going to pay a yearly subscription fee that allows you to host several websites on your account. These fees include the hosting price, domain price, certain plugins that need to be added to the website and any specific themes wanted for a website. Keep these expenses in mind as you set a price for your services.

The good news for web designers and web developers is that pay is very good. These people are some of the highest paid freelancers. This work requires a lot of skill and creativity. That said, if you are a savvy businessperson, can communicate well and have the ability to create amazing websites then you'll be satisfied with your income potential.

As far as time requirement goes, you will most likely be spending a lot of time not only on each project, but also on marketing yourself and keeping up with the latest technology. Depending on how quickly you can plan and build a website, the size of the project plus how specific the client direction is, will determine how long each project may take.

Additional Notes

First tip is very simple: Listen to your client. Clear communication is key. Be sure to ask questions if you don't understand any of their instructions. Consider creating a time schedule for the client so they know when any given milestone will be complete. Be sure you stick to that schedule and if you are unable to do so, tell the client as soon as you know a date will be missed. This is one time surprises are not a good thing. Be open to honest feedback. Under promise and over-deliver! Always exceed your customer's expectations.

Lastly, always be sure to know the necessary tools, programs and skills required to create websites. Keep up with the quickly changing technology. Never stop learning. Dedicate yourself to doing the best job possible every time. And, again, never, ever give up.

Fiverr

Introduction

If you've been reading up to this part, you've probably noticed my reference to Fiverr. Fiverr is one of the more popular platforms aimed at getting freelancers jobs. It brings all of the freelancing work onto one platform. Here, freelancers can advertise their skills so those in need of help can buy their services. Jobs can be sold for anywhere between $5 and $500.

If you are a freelancer now, or are planning on becoming one, it is highly advisable to create an account on their website. Instead of you, the freelancer, applying for work, the customer finds you. It's your responsibility to make yourself and your skills stand out in the crowd. It's another way to look for work. Fiverr is very user friendly and easy to use. Creating a Fiverr account will be well worth the effort.

How To Get Started

Services offered by Fiverr freelancers typically fall under one of nine categories. They are Online Marketing, Writing & Translation, Video & Animation, Music & Audio, Programming & Tech, Advertising, Business and More. So, whether you are a cartoon artist or a financial consultant you probably possess a marketable skill. I suggest going to the site and looking at different profiles not only to see what others are doing, but also what their profiles look like.

Once you decide to use the site, click the "Join" button in the upper right corner. You will then go through several pages filling in your most current information. You can also upload pictures of yourself or something that describes the work you do.

When you're setting up your profile, make sure to sell your services. Don't just list what you do, TELL them what you do. Sell yourself. Differentiate yourself from the competition. Also, make sure you upload samples of previous work completed. Give them something to look at. Remember, you won't have the opportunity to speak to anyone directly, so your profile has to do the talking for you.

After your profile is complete, it's time to start posting responses to "gig requests." Gig requests are posted by employers needing a specific task to be completed and they don't have the time to search through all the profiles looking for exactly what they need. There are several ways to do this. You can create a video or just simply pen a written post. This "ad" tells potential clients what you are able to do for them. It works well to describe the service(s) you are offering, how quickly you can complete the work, your experience and most of all, why they should choose you over someone else. I can't stress this statement enough: It's so important to showcase your skill(s). Now is not the time to be timid or humble.

Once you post a gig response you need to wait for a reply. Do not send multiple responses. When a reply comes, be sure to act quickly. Be polite, professional and nice. Make sure you completely understand what they want done and deliver exactly that back to the client. In fact, I recommend that you exceed your clients' expectations every time. A happy client is your best shot at getting repeat customers and ideally, more "gigs." As you build your list of positive feedback and add to your portfolio, your good reputation will grow. All that's left is to maintain that business and continue to grow.

What To Expect

The good thing with Fiverr is that there are no startup costs. If you have a computer, you can use Fiverr all you want. The only expenses will depend on what service(s) you are offering. Other than that, Fiverr is completely free to sign up and will have you getting gigs in a hurry.

Charging only $5/job isn't going to bring you enough money to pay your bills. However, consider adding "gig extras," to your offering. For example, one musician on Fiverr will create a piano version of your favorite song for $5. For an additional $20, he will add the melody and for an additional $40, he will write the sheet music. So, money you make on Fiverr can act as a major source of your income.

Lastly, the time requirement for this job depends on what services you offer. If you are offering articles for $5, then you won't be spending a lot of time on Fiverr. However, if you get into the bigger job categories, like web development, then you could find yourself taking a lot of time out of your day building websites.

Additional Notes

My first tip when using Fiverr is to load your profile with quality samples of your work. Aside from sounding professional in your profile, be certain to give the clients a large variety of samples to review. If you are confident your work is good, then display every last bit of it. This gives clients an idea of your capabilities. Remember to sell yourself and figure out a way to differentiate yourself from the competition.

.

III. Services

Another easy way to make money with a business created at home is through offering physical services to people. These could be services including but not limited to, tutoring, coaching or day care. This allows you to be your own boss and control how much time you want to spend performing your service.

If you are someone looking for a career similar to having a normal job, but one that doesn't require you to work for someone else, then these are definitely your types of jobs. Although some of them might require certain levels of knowledge, most of them are pretty simple and straight to the point.

Pet Care

Introduction
Pet care can span a wide range of responsibilities. However, if you are a pet lover, then this job could be fun for you. Maybe it won't even feel like work. Customers requiring this service are looking for someone they can trust to come into their home and care for their beloved pet(s). This is probably one of the most appealing jobs in this group of service opportunities. It's hard to hate your job when you staring into the eyes of an adorable puppy or friendly cat.

How To Get Started
To begin you must first decide what pet care services your business is going to offer. There are a wide range of possible services connected to this, including pet sitting, grooming and dog walking. Keep in mind that you'll be the person responsible for cleaning up after that cute puppy or curious cat. That includes pooper scooping and litter box cleaning. In addition you might consider offering additional services like getting the mail or watering plants as a nice extra. Make yourself indispensable to your client when they go out of town.

Next, you need to figure out a name for your business. It should be catchy and engaging to the client. Make it a name that's easy to remember. After your name, it's time to start marketing and promoting your business.

First off, purchase business cards. Make sure you include all pertinent information like cell phone number, website address and maybe even a few services you offer. Consider getting magnetic business cards. Since your name will be stuck to the client's refrigerator it will be easily accessible. Start handing out business cards everywhere. Ask pet stores if you can place a stack of cards on the counter by the cash registers for people to grab. Post your cards on community bulletin boards. Make your name known so people can contact you with potential jobs.

Next on the list is to create a website. In addition to that, establish several social-networking profiles. The internet is a perfect way to promote your business. Create a profile on Facebook and ask friends, family and clients to "like" your page. If pet owners agree, post pictures of the happy pets you've cared for. Consider creating an online newsletter with helpful pet care tips and hints.

When meeting with your clients, dress professionally and be polite. You must establish trust between you and the client, since you will be handling their property while they're gone. Set clear expectations with pet owners so that you both know what services will be provided. Follow through with everything.

Once you have established a solid customer base, offer incentives to happy customers if they refer friends and neighbors to use your service. For example, give them one free day, the next time they book you for five or more days. You want to be continuously building your client list. Be creative.

What To Expect

Startup costs and expenses are going to be common for a pet sitter. First off, if you plan on building a website or buying business cards, you will incur cost. Also, since you're going to have to drive to the client's house, you're going to need to keep track of your mileage in order to claim it as a business expense. You will also need a reliable form of transportation.

As far as income goes, you can expect to make around $32,000 a year[1] working with pet care. Depending on how big your client list is and how well known you are, that number can increase dramatically. There's always the opportunity to expand once you reach enough profit.

The time requirement is going to depend on how many clients you have and the expectations you set. Obviously, if you have many dogs to walk that will probably take more time than feeding, tending to and playing with a cat. Don't forget to take time to keep marketing your service. It's not something you do only once.

Additional Tips

With a job like this, it's important to maintain your professionalism throughout your encounters with your clients. Maintain a positive attitude and be open to feedback. Word of mouth is an excellent way to gain new business. That is, a happy client will be more likely to recommend your services to a friend. Obviously, the more happy clients you have, the more money you make.

Another little tip I can give you when starting a pet care business is to treat the animals with your utmost love and care. No pet owner wants to hire a pet sitter that doesn't treat animals well. Show the owners that you can gain the pet's trust and it will make them feel more comfortable about hiring you.

Daycare/ Baby Sitting

Introduction

If you're an individual that loves to take care of children or babies, then perhaps you've just discovered your next career path. I know there are people out there that love to play with children and teach them how to do their first things. It's an interesting part of life and most people get a kick out of it. What's even more amazing is that a number of parents that are paying people to do these exact things.

If you are interested in opening an at-home daycare and be paid to watch over children and take care of them for a day, an evening or overnight, then you should consider founding a business in that niche. Your passion for caring for children will come through in the work you do then it won't ever feel as if it's a job. Since many households have two parents who work, there is often a need for a caregiver, be it temporary or long-term.

How To Get Started

Becoming a childcare business owner is a serious matter. This means that people will be counting on you to take care of their children while they are away. For that reason, there are a number of licenses and certificates you should get before looking for work. By researching the license requirements for the state in which you live, you can find out which licenses you will need and where to receive those licenses.

After you complete all of the necessary requirements of your state, it is time to name the business you plan on owning. Make a name that is easy to promote and represents your business well. After you find the name, register it with the state and fill out the paperwork to become either a sole proprietorship, a partnership or a corporation. You can do most of that at your state's official website.

Now it's time to establish a price structure that is fair to your clients yet high enough to cover all of your expenses and still make a profit. Expenses could include food for snacks or meals, toys or supplies for activities. Some of that will depend on the ages of the children in your care.

After that, you'll need to advertise. Spread the word about your business and in doing so make sure you mention all the licenses you've obtained. Knowing you are a licensed childcare provider will be a great comfort to parents. Also, make sure to either hire a bookkeeper or establish a record keeping system to keep track of all your business' finances, taxes, income, expenses, etc.

What To Expect

When beginning a childcare business, there will be startup costs and expenses. You need to make sure you have age-appropriate toys and books and possibly even some baby furniture. You'll need to have food that is earmarked solely for childcare use, so it can be claimed as a business expense. Lastly, all of your business cards and website development will cost money. There will be cost associated with licenses too. That will be dependent on the state in which you live.

As far as income goes, you could see yourself making quite a bit of money with this type of business depending on how aggressive your pricing. There is a fine line between making a large profit and making your service affordable to parents. If you are someone who is home during the day and have children of your own, not only will you not have the expense of childcare for your young ones, but you'll be taking in money for the care provide to others.

Lastly, let's talk about how much time will be required to work with this. Anytime you have children in your care you will need to be in business mode. That can get tiring. You'll need to schedule specific dates that you'll be "closed," if you want a break from your business. When signing up for care, your clients will need this information up front so they can plan their schedules around these times. With an in-home business it can get tiring having your home also be the place where you work.

Additional Tips

Okay, this tip may be obvious, but it needs to be stated. Please, if you plan on beginning a business in the childcare niche, please be good with children. If you are short on patience then this is most definitely not the job for you. If you need to, take a couple of classes to help you understand what is involved. It's a huge commitment and is not to be taken lightly. You will be responsible for the safety and well being of someone else's children.

Last piece of advice on this daycare opportunity is to childproof your home. Some of things you do will be requirements to gain certain licenses. For example, covering all of your electrical outlets with outlet covers. Lock cabinets containing cleaning products. Also, put away any special, breakable knickknacks that you treasure. Having a safe environment for the children will not only make you comfortable, but the children will be at ease as well.

Tutoring

Introduction

Another great way to make some extra money with an at-home business is to help students with their schoolwork. If you love learning and have always had a knack for educating, this could be the job for you. You've been teaching your friends for long enough. Why not earn some extra cash while you're at it?

Tutoring is a very simple business. There's not much that goes with it. All you really need is to know the subject you're tutoring very. Basically, if you love to educate others, then you will find great satisfaction while helping kids learn certain subjects.

How To Get Started

There are several steps before you get into the business of tutoring from your home or the students' homes. First off, I would recommend you go to your local school and/or literacy organization. Check with them to see who needs tutoring. This won't give you specific names, but it will give you a general understanding of what age group or area in which the kids need help.

Next, write up a quick contract/agreement that you will use when you start meeting with clients. In the agreement, make sure to outline your expectations as well as your payment plans, prices and schedule. After that is done, it would be smart to gather a business plan. Create a plan of attack, such as the where you will tutor, whom you will tutor and in what subjects you will tutor.

Next up is spreading the word. Get your name out there. Put up flyers around the school and neighborhood. Order some business cards and hand them out at school events.

Go around talking to parents of the school and see if any of their kids need help in a certain area.

Once your name is out there and you have a solid reputation for success, work will begin to gravitate towards you. Tutoring is a constant steady job. There are always kids that struggle with learning that need the extra help and you can be that person.

After you start to get regulars and steady business, just maintain it. However, clients will grow up and graduate, so it is important to keep marketing your business. Word of mouth is a great way to expand this type of business. That is, friends will start recommending your help to others with a need.

What To Expect

Startup costs will include creating and printing flyers and business cards. I would recommend having a computer that is fairly up-to-date since this generation's education is based a lot on the internet. Other expenses might include having supplies like paper, pens, pencils, etc.

As far as income goes, you may see it start very slow. However, it always has the potential to increase. Just be patient. If you find yourself without much business, that just means you need to promote more. Don't be scared to go door to door or to post flyers literally everywhere. Sell yourself.

The time could be substantial. Aside from actually tutoring the kids, which will take a couple hours out of your day per child, you'll have to monitor their improvements and document test scores and the like. Be supportive. Let the child know they have someone who believes in their ability to succeed.

Additional Tips

My first tip is very plain and simple: Stay organized. When you're a tutor, you're always expected to be organized, much like a teacher. A daily scheduling app will come in handy. That way you'll have all the information you need literally at your fingertips.

When keeping track of your time remember that you may need to include travel time if you are tutoring a child in their home. Traffic could interfere with your ability to arrive at a session on time. If you are traveling to a child's home keep detailed mileage records because they can be considered a business expense.

Lastly, remember that this a service job. That means you're providing a service to your client. Your direct client is the student, but don't forget the parent(s). They are the ones who will be paying for your tutoring service. Treat them with respect as well.

Introduction

If you enjoy working out and going to the gym, then listen up. Did you know that you can get paid to lead people in their workouts? Being a fitness coach means you'll be providing personalized fitness coaching to people who want to lose weight, add some muscle or enjoy a healthy lifestyle. Although a lot of testing is involved before becoming a coach, the end result could be satisfying and fun.

You will need proficiency in education, athletic training and knowledge of exercise and health sciences. When becoming a fitness coach, you will be starting as a coach predominantly for amateurs looking to improve their physique. However, you hold the potential to become a fitness coach for professional athletes looking to improve their performance.

How To Get Started

Before you get started as a fitness coach, you should do a little working out yourself. Start with putting together an exercise plan. In addition, take up a healthy diet and maintain that. When you're a fitness coach, you need to reach a level of credibility that makes your clients believe you will help them. Stay healthy, practice what you preach and you will start to become a great fitness coach.

Next, it is recommended that you hire your own fitness coach. It doesn't have to be for long. It could only be for a month or so. This is a good thing to do for two reasons. First, you will see yourself improve physically, which is always good. Second, you will get a sneak peek into some of the techniques used by professional fitness coaches. You gain insight and garner ideas for ways you can inspire your own clients.

Next up, I would recommend taking some classes for fitness coaching. I would say your best bet is to find a local college or university that offers classes and get into some of those. Develop a solid foundation for this profession and make sure you know as much as possible about it. Aspire to be the best fitness coach out there.

Next, you need to launch your business. Start small and offer fitness coaching to your friends and family. Then start to ask your neighbors. Check around for your competitor's prices and try to offer your clients a reduced price. Promote your new business, by putting up flyers and giving away business cards. Go to nutrition or vitamin stores and see if they will let you put your information at their cash register. Get your name out there so people know you exist.

Once you're ready to kick it into high gear, sign up for your certification through the National Athletic Trainer's Association Board of Certification. After you pass the test and become a certified trainer, you can start training clients. You can start solo and then build by hiring more trainers once business gets booming.

What To Expect

Your startup costs are going to include any memberships to a gym you use, the cost to make flyers and print business cards and any gas money needed to get to and from the gym. You'll also spend a lot of money on protein and mass gainers or any vitamins you take. Chances are, you'll be taking a lot of these supplements and it's no secret that they're expensive.

As far as income goes, this is yet another steady business. There's always a group of people that want to get back in shape and are willing to pay someone to help. Once your client list grows, you may see them recommend you to friends they know.

This could be a full time endeavor and you'll be spending a lot of time in your "office" the gym. Working out isn't for everyone, but if it is your passion and you enjoy helping others meet their goals, this is a good choice for a small business. However, if you're going to be a fitness coach, you probably will need to get used to a lot of sore days and tired nights.

Additional Tips

First off, I would recommend you get some kind of a day planner. Once you start to get customers, you're going to need to keep track of appointments. A day planner is inexpensive and will be one of your most handy tools. You'll see yourself checking it every day just like your phone.

My next tip is to simply respect your clients. They need your support. If they hired you, it means they need help reaching a goal. You're there to inspire them to keep going and be their inspiration to do better. Typically, positive reinforcement works better than negative comments. Also, I imagine that when you help a client reach a goal, you will experience a high yourself.

Conclusion

As you can see there are many opportunities to support yourself with a business of your own. From selling things on eBay or Amazon Marketplace, to tapping into your creativity by starting a blog or learning to design web sites. If you don't consider yourself tech savvy, maybe a dog walking service or babysitting gig is preferable. My goal for this book is to show you that opportunities exist. And, don't limit yourself. Maybe you have an idea that isn't listed here. That does not mean it's not valid. Explore. Discover. Try. Learn. The information in this book is presented to you as way to inspire you to think differently. It doesn't give you every detail on every business opportunity, but rather, enough information to determine if a certain path could be right for you. Find what works for you. The life of a freelancer is possible. Be thoughtful as you move forward, knowing that any road you choose will have challenges. Hopefully, you can surround yourself with people who support your vision. If not, find groups of like-minded business owners for encouragement. Know that I support you in whatever you do and want only the greatest success in your future. I believe in you!

Your Free Gift

I wanted to show my appreciation that you support my work so I've put together a free gift for you.

Business Startup Resource Toolkit

Just visit the link below to download it now.

http://zenmagicpublishing.com/hbb

Thanks!

Zachary Grayson

Endnotes

---

[1] FreeMoneyFinance website. "Dog Walking, Pet Sitting, and the Money You Can Make." May 18, 2009.

www.ingramcontent.com/pod-product-compliance
Lightning Source LLC
Chambersburg PA
CBHW051257170526
45165CB00004B/1748

*9 7 8 1 5 0 2 4 6 1 8 0 3 *